Six Themes Everyone Should Know

Exodus

V. Steven Parrish

Geneva
Press

© 2019 Geneva Press

First edition
Published by Geneva Press
Louisville, Kentucky

19 20 21 22 23 24 25 26 27 28—10 9 8 7 6 5 4 3 2 1

All rights reserved. Except where permission to photocopy is expressly granted on the material, no part of these materials may be reproduced or transmitted in any form or by any means, electronic or mechanical, including photocopying, recording, or by any information storage or retrieval system, without permission in writing from the publisher. For information, address Geneva Press, 100 Witherspoon Street, Louisville, Kentucky 40202-1396.

Unless otherwise indicated, Scripture quotations are from the New Revised Standard Version of the Bible, © 1989 by the Division of Christian Education of the National Council of the Churches of Christ in the U.S.A., and used by permission. In some instances, adaptations have been made to a Scripture or a confession to make the language inclusive.

Excerpts from the *Book of Order* and *Book of Confessions* have been used throughout this resource. Both are reprinted with permission of the Office of the General Assembly.

Cover designer: Rebecca Kueber

Library of Congress Cataloging-in-Publication Data

Names: Parrish, V. Steven, 1953- author.
Title: Six themes in Exodus everyone should know / V. Steven Parrish.
Description: First edition. | Louisville, Kentucky : Geneva Press, 2019. |
  Series: Six themes everyone should know series
Identifiers: LCCN 2019001549 (print) | LCCN 2019016979 (ebook) | ISBN
  9781611649536 (ebk.) | ISBN 9781571532435 (pbk. : alk. paper)
Subjects: LCSH: Bible. Exodus--Theology.
Classification: LCC BS1245.52 (ebook) | LCC BS1245.52 .P37 2019 (print) |
  DDC 222/.1206--dc23
LC record available at https://lccn.loc.gov/2019001549

Most Geneva Press books are available at special quantity discounts when purchased in bulk by corporations, organizations, and special-interest groups. For more information, please e-mail SpecialSales@GenevaPress.com.

Contents

Listing of *Six Themes Everyone Should Know* series iv
Introduction to the *Six Themes Everyone Should Know* series v
Introduction to *Exodus* vi
Biblical Backgrounds to Exodus vii
1. God Listens 1
2. God Responds 7
3. God Engages Human Agents 15
4. God Sustains 23
5. God Is Present 31
6. God Is Merciful and Gracious 39
Group Gatherings, by Eva Stimson 47
    Group Gathering 1 49
    Group Gathering 2 53
    Group Gathering 3 57
    Group Gathering 4 61
    Group Gathering 5 65
    Group Gathering 6 69
Glossary 73
Want to Know More? 75

Six Themes Everyone Should Know series

The Bible, by Barry Ensign-George
Genesis, by W. Eugene March
Matthew, by James E. Davison
Luke, by John T. Carroll
1 and 2 Timothy, by Thomas G. Long
Jeremiah, by W. Eugene March
Exodus, by V. Steven Parrish

Introduction to the
Six Themes Everyone Should Know series

The *Six Themes Everyone Should Know* series focuses on the study of Scripture. Bible study is vital to the lives of churches. Churches need ways of studying Scripture that can fit a variety of contexts and group needs. *Six Themes Everyone Should Know* studies offer a central feature of church adult educational programs. Their flexibility and accessibility make it possible to have short-term studies that introduce biblical books and their main themes.

Six Themes Everyone Should Know consists of six chapters that introduce major biblical themes. At the core of each chapter is an introduction and three major sections. These sections relate to key dimensions of Bible study. These sections ask:
- What does this biblical theme mean?
- What is the meaning of this biblical theme for the life of faith?
- What does this biblical theme mean for the church at this point in history for action?

This format presents a compact and accessible way for people in various educational settings to gain knowledge about major themes in the biblical books; to experience the impact of what Scripture means for Christian devotion to God; and to consider ways Scripture can lead to new directions for the church in action.

Introduction to *Exodus*

Exodus is one of the books of the Pentateuch, the first five books of the Old Testament. The opening verses describe a continuation of creational and covenantal themes in Genesis. Long years after their arrival in Egypt and the death of Joseph, the Israelites have grown "exceedingly strong, so that the land was filled with them" (Exodus 1:7), just as God had promised (Genesis 1:28; 35:1).

The tone turns ominous when the story introduces "a new king [who] arose over Egypt, who did not know Joseph" (Exodus 1:8). Pharaoh perceives a threat to his state economy, so he enslaves the Israelites. Thus, an oppressive power, bolstered by the gods of Egypt, threatens the promises God made to the ancestors and the whole of creation. And so the dramatic conflict is set. What follows is a tale that has emboldened oppressed people for centuries, a story in which God empowers human striving for freedom.

In this insightful study, Steven Parrish introduces us to six themes that focus on revealing the character of God. God listens to the captives' suffering and responds with a name (YHWH) and several emissaries. From the Passover meal through the wilderness, God sustains the people with food, water, and law. God promises to be present to the people in the gifts of the tabernacle and the Ark of the Covenant. Finally, God is merciful and gracious, as demonstrated in the golden calf episode.

May this study fill your heart with confidence in the promises and purposes of the God of the Exodus.

Biblical Backgrounds to Exodus

Author and Date
"My own point of view is that Exodus is a patchwork quilt of traditions from various periods in Israel's life. Yet it is also a finished product. In its earliest form, it was probably a relatively brief narrative with the basic thread of the story, dating before the monarchy. . . . Existing versions of the story were reworked and supplemented in a major way during the exile by a redactor."
—Terence E. Fretheim, *Exodus*, Interpretation: A Bible Commentary for Teaching and Preaching (Louisville, KY: Westminster John Knox Press, 1991), 5–6.

Major Concerns
"God does not remain unchanged by all that happens. . . . God is not only the one who is; God is also one who in some sense becomes. Hence the identity of Yahweh, not very clear at the beginning of the narrative, achieves a depth and clarity as the narrative progresses through divine speech and action as well as human alertness and boldness."
—Fretheim, *Exodus*, 15.

"The exodus is seen to be a sign of hope that poverty and oppression are not the last word, for God is at work on behalf of a different future."
—Fretheim, *Exodus*, 18.

Importance
"The book of Exodus moves from slavery to worship, from Israel's bondage to Pharaoh to its bonding to Yahweh."
—Fretheim, *Exodus*, 1.

"As a constitutive event, the exodus . . . so captured the imagination of Israel that it not only served to illuminate Israel's most basic identity but also functioned as a prism for interpreting all of Israel's subsequent history."
—Fretheim, *Exodus*, 10.

God not only speaks and acts but also listens.

Chapter 1
God Listens

Scripture
Exodus 1-2   God listens to captive people.
Exodus 15:22-25; 16:1-17:7   God listens to hungry and thirsty people.
Exodus 32:1-14; 33:7-11   God listens to intercessory prayers.

Prayer
God, there are so many words—too many. Everyone is talking, and no one listens. Sometimes it feels like what we have to say—yearn to say, need to say—is squeezed out because of so many words. But you have shown yourself, again and again, to be a listening God who hears our outcries, even welcomes them. And more, we have found healing in your listening, and we thank you. Help us to become engaged listeners too, and perhaps as we listen to others, we may become agents of healing. Amen.

Introduction
The opening of the book of Exodus is tightly linked to the preceding book of Genesis. Exodus 1:1-5 reminds us that Jacob and his family, to whom we are introduced in Genesis, have made their way to Egypt. We quickly discover that by the time of the Exodus narrative the first generation of Israelite sojourners has died, but not before being faithful to the creational mandate to "be fruitful

and multiply" (Genesis 1:28). Clearly, God has been faithful to the promises made to Abraham, Isaac, and Jacob (12:2; 15:5; 17:6; 26:4; 28:14). They indeed have many descendants, as Exodus 1:7 makes clear. Unfortunately, the descendants reside not in the land of the promise but in Egypt. The story of Exodus will set into motion the events that will eventually bring together the twin pillars of God's commitment to the ancestors: land and descendants.

The Israelites' abundant growth does not go unnoticed. A new, unnamed Pharaoh sees and, alarmed by Israel's creative potential, sets in place policies designed to thwart the reproductive capabilities of the people. First comes the policy of severe and oppressive labor. When that fails, Pharaoh commands that all newborn male children be executed. Then, the people "cried out" (Exodus 2:23).

The narrative does not say that the people cried out to God. We know only that they "cried out," and that God heard. Perhaps "overheard" would be more precise. God's hearing leads to divine remembering and reminds God of the pledge to the ancestors of descendants and land—a guarantee now threatened by the reckless and deadly policies of Pharaoh. God's hearing or listening sets the exodus into motion.

The outcry of the people will have a joyful counterpart in Exodus 15. After the people are beyond the sea safely out of reach of Pharaoh, Moses and Miriam will sing songs of thanksgiving. Thus, the first significant section of Exodus has an almost lament-like structure: outcry, petitions along the way, and finally affirmation with thanksgiving. All are predicated on a God who listens.

A Basic Theme: God Listens

For faith communities the actions and speech of God have held central focus when reading Exodus. After all, the Hebrew word *dabar* translates as both word and act. For a period in the twentieth century, it was customary for both the church and the academy to view the bulk of the Old Testament as a witness to the mighty acts of God in history. Although that view has fallen out of favor, it is beyond question that the Bible portrays a God who acts and speaks. That it also presents a God who listens has been less noticed.

The theme of divine listening is painted against the backdrop of human outcry, complaint, petition, and inquiry. In each case, God's attentive capacity is on bold display.

Outcry. As noted above, Israel's initial outcry is a tormented outpouring of anguish to whomever might hear. Perhaps the reader is supposed to infer that the cry was explicitly directed to God, but the text itself is not quite that bold. It will be later, at the crossing of the sea, when the narrator tells us that the Israelites "cried out to the LORD" (Exodus 14:10). But here it is the unfocused outcry of people in misery that God hears.

Complaint. In Exodus 16 the people are between the sea and Sinai when they begin to "complain" or "grumble" because they are hungry. This complaint was explicitly directed against Moses and Aaron (16:2). The people reason that it would have been better to have stayed in Egypt where food and water were readily available. Although Moses deftly deflects their complaint and counters that the people were, in fact, complaining against God, the Lord hears and provides the gift of manna (16:12). While the people's complaining will be treated differently in Numbers, here the Lord realizes that food and water are crucial for their survival and responds accordingly.

Petition. One of the more visible ways in which God's listening is crucial is in petition. It was Moses' speaking to God ("crying out") that resulted in fresh water (15:22–25). More pointedly, following the golden calf episode (32:1–6), God is said to be genuinely angry: ". . . that my wrath may burn hot against them and I may consume them" (32:10). In a shrewdly crafted intercession, Moses argues that God's honor will be tarnished should God give full vent to divine wrath. As a result of divine listening, the destruction of the "calf builders" was graciously averted.

Inquiry. In Exodus 33:7–11 readers are suddenly and unexpectedly introduced to the tent of meeting. People who sought the Lord would go there, presumably to inquire about some matter. Moses would enter the tent, where he and God would have a conversation, much as friends talk to one another (v. 11). To be sure, the text talks about God speaking, but the notions of inquiry and conversation suggest very strongly that the God of the tent and the God of Exodus is a listening God.

The Life of Faith: God Listens to Us

While the Exodus affirmation that God listens may be a theme in a biblical book, it is much more than that. It is also a mark of the fundamental character of God. To put it another way, when God listens, God is acting in character. More importantly, the God we encounter in Exodus is the same Holy One who journeys with us by day and watches over us at night. The God who heard the outcry of oppressed slaves in the past is the same God who hears us and stands bound to us in covenant fidelity today. That is good news!

That the Lord listens means that God is accessible. There are no lines in which to wait, no passports, visas, voter I.D.'s, P.I.N.'s, or passwords. All that's necessary is a cry, a complaint, a petition, or an inquiry. Accessibility to God flows from the Holy One's character as a listening God.

The dependability of a listening God stands in stark contrast to the world that many of us experience day in and day out. The polarization that exists between political parties, factions within parties, the various "culture wars," radical disagreements over immigration, and so on are often driven by loud and angry voices shouting at and past one another. Genuine dialogue and conversation rarely take place. Unlike the exchanges between Moses and God in the tent of meeting, we've become accustomed to gall and bitterness. For many people of faith, it has become an alien and disorienting world. Surely the world from which the Israelites cried out also seemed strange and disorienting. After all, Egypt was a land that once offered food and life, but new leaders transformed it into a land of oppression and death. From that context, God heard, and the events that led to liberation were set into motion. So there is a reason for us to have hope.

Finally, events and crises in life overtake us, and it seems that there is no one to whom to turn. A child lies dying in a hospital bed. A young teenager is bullied at school and on social media. A husband of fifty years is slowly slipping away into the darkness of dementia. A young mother is sinking into the depths of depression. A young husband is ensnared by the deadly grip of opioid addiction. The list seems endless, and in so many of these cases, it can seem that there is no one to whom to turn—or at least no one who is up to the task at hand.

The only petition in the desperate Psalm 88 is "Let my prayer come before you; incline your ear to my cry" (v. 2). This is a prayer that pleads to be heard from the depths of utter despair. The good news from the Exodus story is that God hears us and listens to us.

The Church: A Listening Community

In many ways, the church is a community of prayer. That is as it should be. As a community organized around the presence of God, prayer should be a central part of its life. So, no less than individuals, the church cries out, complains, petitions, and inquires. And just as God listens to individuals, God listens to the church at prayer. In fact, prayer is predicated on the theological conviction that God listens and has the freedom and wisdom to choose if and how to respond. If that were not the case, then prayer would make little sense. And so we pray, "Lord, hear our prayer."

If the conviction of a listening God beckons us to pray, might there be another side to this "theological coin"? If the church is to sense anything instructive for its nature and being from the biblical portrayal of God, should we not be about this business of listening as well?

The church has not always been keen on listening. We have been far more focused on speaking. We have often attended to rules and regulations: what to do or not to do; who's right or wrong. We've made pronouncements about orthodoxy or heresy, producing creeds and confessions. Not that these are necessarily inappropriate for the church, but what if we flipped the coin? What would it be like to become a genuine, listening community? What might the church look like if it decided, instead of speaking first and listening later, to listen along with God?

One of the many things that the #MeToo and Black Lives Matter movements have shown us is that there are people all around us whose voices have not been heard. One can only suspect that these are the tip of the iceberg. Tragic incidents of harassment and overt racism created contexts in which hurting people found a voice and are finally being heard. But must it take a tragedy to create a space for oppressed people to be heard? Are there not ways that the church can offer safe places for anguished and hurt people to cry out, without being judgmental or patronizing? Sometimes merely being heard is enough to provide at least a toehold on life.

With a little imagination, a lot of patience, and a lot of effort, surely the church can learn the art of listening.

If the church is to be a genuine healing agent in a broken world, then those of us who are the church are enjoined to develop our capacity to listen along with God. We are beckoned to identify the people whose voices have been stifled for one reason or the other. The challenge, then, is to create the space and opportunity for the hurting people among us to shout out and be heard instead of being dismissed. That is the path that leads from brokenness to wholeness and well-being. That is the Exodus path.

For Reflection and Action
1. Have you ever experienced a sense of relief—even healing—when someone has sincerely listened to share your concerns?

2. Identify specific people or groups in your community who cry out to be heard. What are their interests?

3. Name ways that your congregation can be a better listener. What are some specific ways that you can make your church a safe and caring community where people feel comfortable voicing their most profound concerns?

4. Create a puzzle in which children fill in key words or phrases pertaining to themes of "God listens." Share the puzzle with the children in your church.

God responds to Israel's cries because God is bound to it through an ancient covenant made with Abraham, Isaac, and Jacob.

Chapter 2

God Responds

Scripture
Exodus 6:1–13 God establishes a covenant and makes a people.

Exodus 6:28–12:32 God and Pharaoh vie for control of the people.

Exodus 14 God opens the sea and leads the people from bondage to freedom.

Prayer
Gracious Lord, you have pledged to be our God and have called us to be your people. Bound to you in the covenant, we are bold to call out to you in praise and in need. We are thankful that you not only hear our prayers but that you have both the power and inclination to respond. You have brought us through deep waters in the past, and we trust your guidance now and in the future. When our backs are against the wall, and all seems lost, your sure and certain help sees us through. We give you thanks. Amen.

Introduction
While listening is an essential characteristic of God, it is by no means all there is to the Holy One. God also responds. For some, this claim may sound like a truism. Indeed, the entire Exodus narrative has sometimes been viewed as one in which God responds

to the outcry of Israel. Nothing much new there, it would seem. For others, to speak of "God Responds" as a theme may appear much too broad to be helpful. However, two subthemes help give nuance to the larger theme of "God Responds":

God responds as the covenant keeper. God responds as the one who remains faithful to the ancient covenant made with the ancestors. The occasional mention of Abraham, Isaac, and Jacob by name (for example, Exodus 2:24; 3:6; 3:16; 4:5; 6:3) and the recurring designation of Israel as "my people" are reminders of the covenant between God and Israel. This covenant relationship prompts God to act on behalf of Israel; it will be severely strained at times, but it will hold.

God responds as the Creator. Biblical interpreters have often focused mostly on the opening chapters of Genesis when speaking of God's creative activity. But God's activity as Creator is by no means limited to those chapters of the Bible. Thanks especially to the work of Old Testament scholar Terence Fretheim[1] it has become clear that creation theology permeates, if not undergirds, the larger Exodus narrative.

In these two subthemes, God acts both for the sake of Israel and for the sake of the world. That is, God's Genesis promise to Abraham (and, hence, Israel) was that Abraham/Israel would be blessed and also be a blessing to the world. Both Israel and the larger world are in view in the old promise. God is both the creator of the world and, through the exodus, the maker of Israel. The covenantal promises to the ancestors and God's work as Creator are tightly interwoven in God's response to Israel's cry.

A Basic Theme: God Responds

God responds to Israel's outcry as covenant keeper. God's response presupposes a previous arrangement with the ancestors and an ongoing relationship with their descendants (cf. Genesis 12:1-2; 15:17-21; 17:1-2; especially Exodus 2:2-4; 3:6; 6:2-13). The recipients of divine aid in the Exodus story are not just any

---

1. Terence E. Fretheim, *Exodus*, Interpretation: A Bible Commentary for Teaching and Preaching (Louisville, KY: Westminster John Knox Press, 1991).

old group of oppressed slaves. They are a particular lot: God's people. The expression "my people" (Hebrew, *'ammi*) appears frequently in Exodus (for example, 3:7, 10; 5:1; 7:16; 8:1, 13, 20; 10:3). The wording that appears in Exodus 6:7 is slightly different (literally, "I will take you to me for a people"), but the meaning is the same. The objects of God's response in Exodus are the people to whom God is deeply bound by covenant.

The one time in the book of Exodus—perhaps the whole Pentateuch—when the unique relationship between Israel and God seems most in peril is the golden calf incident (Exodus 32). In the lengthy absence of Moses, the people have Aaron fashion a calf image and attribute their deliverance to it instead of Israel's God, the Lord. As can happen in any relationship, God is understandably angered. God threatens to obliterate the people and make Moses great instead. Here God does not use the familiar designation "my people" but says to Moses they are "your people" (v. 7). Moses challenges God; he counters that they are not his people but indeed God's people (v. 11). Although there are consequences for the people's actions, there is not wholesale obliteration. Even in the face of painful betrayal, God remains the covenant keeper.

God responds as Creator. The book of Exodus opens with a telling observation: "The Israelites were fruitful and prolific; they multiplied and grew exceedingly strong so that the land was filled with them" (1:7). Israel had indeed been faithful to the creational mandate of Genesis 1:28: "'Be fruitful and multiply, and fill the earth . . .'" (see also, 9:1, 7)! Frightened by the creative capacity of Israel, Pharaoh seeks to thwart it by toilsome work and murder (Exodus 1:8–22). Pharaoh thus stands in opposition to the Lord's creational intentions. Because of Pharaoh's unwillingness to yield to God's command "Let my people go," the order that was established initially at creation is disrupted by the various "plagues" (7:14–12:32). The crossing of the sea in Exodus 14 recalls Genesis 1, where the spirit/wind "swept over the face of the waters" (Genesis 1:2), setting into motion the appearance of an ordered world. In Exodus, the wind blows upon the waters of the sea, resulting in the appearance of dry land upon which Israel escapes from the death-dealing Egyptians. Subsequently God rains down "'bread from heaven'" (Exodus 16:4) and provides water in the wilderness (Exodus 17).

Throughout the whole Exodus story, God's creational power is on display. While this is a part of God's response to Israel's outcry, the Creator also acts on behalf of the entire world under siege by Pharaoh's chaotic actions. God responds as Creator.

The Life of Faith: Living in Covenant with the Creator

For many people today the notion of covenant may seem an odd, or even alien, idea. Except for an occasional mention in church, or perhaps at a wedding, the word *covenant* rarely comes up. We're far more familiar with expressions like "memorandums of agreement," "contracts," or other similar legal arrangements. Contracts and other agreements usually have "out clauses"—grounds on which one contractual partner (usually the one in power) may terminate the contract. Not so with the covenant between God and God's people. God is in a committed relationship with us. We may hurt, disappoint, even anger God, but the divine covenant keeper will not forsake us. God will not walk out the door.

We are surrounded by impermanence these days. Jobs are often viewed as stepping stones to better jobs. Executives move employees from state to state to satisfy corporate needs. Marriages, where the word *covenant* is right at home, frequently end in bitterness and divorce. Children grow up and move to other cities. Everything and everyone is on the move. Dislocation and vertigo are the norms. In such a world as ours, knowing that God the covenant keeper is committed to each one of us can be an anchor that holds us steady.

To trust that God is in a committed relationship with each of us also serves as a guide for how we relate to other people. Our co-workers become more than competition or threats. Our friends and family members are not viewed as people who merely exist to serve us in some way or boost our ego. Others with whom we disagree—or may not even like—are not viewed as enemies to be overcome. To engage others as covenant partners leads us to find ways to support, encourage, and empower our peers and families day after day.

The One who has entered into a covenant with us is the "maker of heaven and earth." To be in a committed relationship with the Creator is no small matter!

Isaiah 40–55 seems to reflect Judah's experience of the Babylonian exile (597–538 BCE). Removed from their homeland and deprived of Jerusalem, the Temple, and their Davidic king, the Judeans were beaten down and caught up in despair. Filled with questions of whether or not the Lord was still in control, the prophet—profoundly influenced by creation and exodus traditions—frequently spoke of the creative power of God:

> Who has measured the waters in the hollow of his hand
>   and marked off the heavens with a span,
> enclosed the dust of the earth in a measure,
>   and weighed the mountains in scales
>   and the hills in a balance? (Isaiah 40:12)

The answer, of course, is the Lord. The same God who parted the sea and led Israel to safety so long ago is surely able to lead us out of the exile and back to our homes. This is none other than the Creator, our own covenant partner.

The Church: God's People

Moses meets God twice in the opening chapters of Exodus. Chapter 3, the more intimate encounter, contains the burning bush episode. During his exchange with the voice from the bush, Moses asks for the name of the One calling to him. The voice gives a name, but it is cryptic: YHWH, the Lord.[2] Moses is given the responsibility of being the agent through whom God will work to liberate Israel. Following a mysterious encounter with YHWH on his way back to Egypt (Exodus 4) and an unsuccessful first attempt to free the slaves (Exodus 5), Moses meets the Lord again (Exodus 6). Chapters 3 and 6 may originally have been two separate traditions about the revelation of the divine name, but here they bookend a fearful experience and a failed attempt to gain Israel's freedom that results only in harder work (bricks without straw!) and the people's anger (Exodus 5:21).

---

2. When English scholars translate this Hebrew word they typically render it using all capital letters: the LORD.

The second iteration of the divine name in Exodus 6:1–9 is noteworthy for its threefold repetition of the statement, "'I am the LORD'" (vv. 2, 6, 8). In the wake of fear and apparent failure, God reminds Moses of the One who stands beside him. This One has chosen Israel as "'my people,'" pledged to be their God, and will guide them into the land of the promise despite all odds (Exodus 6:7–8).

For many in the church, the times in which we live are uncertain and unsettling. Declining membership, congregations closing, dwindling financial resources, decreasing enrollment in seminaries—these and so many other realities are indeed formidable. It is essential to be reminded from time to time, as was Moses, that in the face of fear and failure we do not stand alone, for the Lord is with us. This is the God who stands as covenant keeper and creator, in whom we can have faith and on whom we can surely depend.

The sea, which stood between Israel's almost certain death and their deliverance, also must have seemed formidable. Moses instructed the people to "'stand firm'" (Exodus 14:13). A bit later the narrative tells us that the Lord caused a wind (Hebrew *ruach*; wind, spirit) to blow throughout the night to divide the waters and create a way out for Israel.

There is a message for the church in this account: Stand firm. Standing firm means standing firm in faithfulness to the Lord while remaining open to the spirit and the new work that God, covenant keeper and Creator, is able to do for all of God's people. Fear and potential failure will always be real possibilities. But we do not face them by ourselves. God listens, and God responds.

For Reflection and Action

1. In what ways or places do you experience covenantal promises in your life? Is covenant limited only to church matters (for example, church and wedding vows), or does it extend to other areas of life?

2. When speaking to an unrepentant Israel, Amos delivered this divine message: "You only have I known of all the families of the earth; therefore I will punish you for all your iniquities" (Amos 3:2). What does this suggest about the nature of covenant?

3. Name ways that you have experienced the intervention of God in your life. Was God's presence disorienting or reorienting, or some of both?

4. Choose from this chapter's Scripture readings a verse that can be a reminder for covenant faithfulness, and write that verse on an index card that can be kept in a conspicuous place as a daily reminder.

The story of Exodus opens with the narrative of five women, all of whom are going about normal activities of life.

Chapter 3

God Engages Human Agents

Scripture
Exodus 1:15–2:10   Women subvert the deadly plans of Pharaoh.

Exodus 3:1–12   God calls and sends Moses.

Exodus 4:10; 6:28–9:13   God appoints Aaron to be Moses' spokesman.

Prayer
Thank you, God, for gifts and the opportunities to use them. You have endowed each of us with unique talents, abilities, and vision, and you beckon us to use them for the well-being of all your people, all your world. We confess that sometimes we fail to use our gifts wisely. At other times we are timid and hesitant to use them. But you have called us and have promised to be with us through our successes and our failures. Embolden and empower us to be your faithful agents in a very needy world. Amen.

Introduction
It can be tempting to approach the book of Exodus as a story of God's deeds to liberate Israel. Such an approach would not be entirely mistaken, although it would fail to capture the full and rich textures of the larger story. In addition to divine action, God also engages various aspects of the creation itself and draws them

into the work of deliverance. In particular, God engages human beings as agents of divine intervention.

As a general rule of interpretation, the Bible does not speak of God in an abstract or purely philosophical fashion. For example, the words *omnipotence, omniscience,* and *omnipresence*—terms that some interpreters like to throw out in their "God speak"—are not at home in the biblical text. We learn of God from the way that the Holy One interacts with the world and its creatures. Usually, that divine interaction is not a heavy-handed one, especially when it comes to human beings. In many cases, God seems perfectly willing to change the divine mind after engaging with human agents (for example, Exodus 32:11–14; cf. also Amos 7:1–6). So, throughout the Exodus story, God solicits human agents to assist in the immense task of liberation.

With that said, God's inclination to work with and through human agents should not lead to the extreme claim, as sometimes happens, that we are the only hands that God has. The God we encounter in the Bible is more than capable of acting without human assistance. Look no further than the opening chapters of Genesis to see God at work well before humans are around. Or, a quick read of the story about the Ark of the Covenant in 1 Samuel 4–6 will make clear that "the hand of the Lord" is able to act on its own! Still, God has made humans with creative leadership capacities (Genesis 1:26–28) and chooses to include them in God's involvement with the world. In Exodus, humans can act in ways that support God's creational desire without being directly instructed, or they can act as a result of the divine call. But act they do.

A Basic Theme: God Engages Human Agents

Exodus opens with a list of names (all male) that connects what follows with what has transpired in Genesis. In fact, the Hebrew title for Exodus is "These are the names." Very quickly the book turns attention to a character that is never named: Pharaoh. Scholars suspect that the historical person behind this moniker is Rameses II, to be dated in the thirteenth century BCE. The text refuses to utter the name of Egypt's ruler. That he is nameless does not mean he is powerless. Indeed, this unnamed king reveals himself to be shrewd, ruthless, and a bit paranoid. Fearful of Israel's creative capacity, Pharaoh orders policies intended to stifle Israel's emerging presence: hard labor and male infanticide.

Two named women. Into this deadly crisis, two women are introduced. Unlike Pharaoh, they have names: Shiphrah and Puah. Unlike Pharaoh, who deals in death, they are midwives whose vocation is life. We do not know if they were Hebrew or Egyptian, although the irony would be great indeed if they were Egyptian! We do know that they defy Pharaoh's command to kill all newborn male babies. Nowhere are we told that God specifically instructed them to act in this manner. We know only that they feared God (Exodus 1:17) and chose life over death, and that God "dealt well with [them]" (Exodus 1:20). On what the women knew about God, the text also remains silent. Nevertheless, their agency was precisely aligned with God's creative design for Israel.

Three unnamed women. The next episode (Exodus 2:1–10) drives daringly toward the name that will dominate the rest of the story: Moses. While the actions of the midwives have prevented the immediate death of male babies, there is no guarantee of their continued survival. So when a Levite's wife gives birth to a boy, the mother places her son in a basket (Hebrew, *tebat,* the same word used for Noah's ark) and set him adrift on a river. His sister (usually assumed to be Miriam but here unnamed) follows. In a moment of grand irony, she witnesses the daughter of Pharaoh rescue a Hebrew baby her father wants to kill! The sister negotiates to find a wet nurse for the child, who turns out to be the infant's mother. He will be returned upon weaning to the household of Pharaoh, which he will eventually bring down! Irony abounds! Nowhere is God mentioned in the episode, and the reader is again left to ponder whether or not the hand of providence guides the events.

Moses. God's voice from the bush is clear and signals God's awareness of Israel's plight and the divine intention to help. In a stunning move, God says to Moses, "'I will send you'" (Exodus 3:10). To every excuse Moses offers to decline, God has a response: a name (3:13–15), a staff (4:1–5), and a spokesman (4:10–17).

Aaron. Aaron was the first priest of ancient Israel. He was the older brother of Moses, born into the tribe of Levi. Aaron is first mentioned in Exodus 4:14 when God, angry that Moses made excuses for refusing the mission to free Israel from bondage, appointed Aaron to be Moses' spokesman. Aaron accompanied Moses and the Israelites as they journeyed in the wilderness.

God engages human agents.

The Life of Faith: Vocations for All

A vocation typically involves an alignment between a person's gifts and talents and a perceived need that strongly attracts that person. The alignment need not be perfect, and rarely is. However, the attraction, the calling, to undertake a particular task is the hallmark of a vocation.

Often people say, "I don't have any gifts, or if I do, I don't know what they are." But gifts come in all kinds of packages. Sometimes abilities that seem average and insignificant can lead to immense blessing.

Shiphrah and Puah were doing their jobs as midwives by helping women deliver babies. While they likely had training, the text doesn't comment on their medical credentials. They quietly went about their work. Their typical work becomes extraordinary when the two named women defy the order of the unnamed Pharaoh. They refused to kill the male babies upon birth. Then, under interrogation by the Pharaoh, they used their wits (lied?!) to avoid punishment. The only credential that the text mentions (twice) is that they "feared God." Their bold actions based on their stance toward God transformed their regular work into a life-saving vocation.

Three unnamed women in Exodus 2:1–10 were going about ordinary things: giving birth, watching after a younger sibling, taking a bath. But the ordinary becomes extraordinary along the way. A mother places her newborn in a basket released upon a river; an Egyptian princess knowingly rescues a Hebrew baby boy; a bold sister negotiates a wet nurse for the infant. Three women caught up in their usual roles audaciously defy the deadly mandate of Pharaoh and become extraordinary in so doing.

Moses was doing his regular work of shepherding for his father-in-law. It was probably not the most exciting work in the world. But out of nowhere, God flags Moses down and gives him a different flock to shepherd (Exodus 3-4). To be sure, Moses seems to have preferred four-legged sheep over the two-legged variety and makes full admission to God of his limitations. But God is determined, and off go Moses and his brother Aaron to Egypt. Ordinary, mundane work is transformed into a life-saving vocation.

And so it is with us as people of faith. The universal vocation of being human and bearing the image of God is sufficient. Times and situations will arise that beckon us to step forward in response to a need. The answer we make may be as small as a smile, a hug, a kind word, or a listening ear. But small gestures like these often lead to transformational moments. To be sure, we may fail. Moses and Aaron failed multiple times in their efforts to free Israel. But the need kept calling them, and God's urging led them to continue until finally, Israel was released. So we should not buckle in our resolve when our best efforts are met with apparent failures. Such can be the life of faith.

The Church: Engaged and Engaging

The presence of Moses looms large in Exodus—so large, in fact, that it can be tempting to overlook that Moses is part of a broader community. While God engages individual human agents, God also engages groups of human agents. The groups may not always be large; however, large or small, God draws on groups to advance divine purposes.

Two midwives worked together to preserve lives. Three women worked together to rescue the infant Moses. In this instance, each provided something that the other couldn't. One had the power to save that the others did not have. Another had the knowledge and ability to bring the princess and the wet nurse together. Finally, two brothers together, Moses and Aaron, were sent to Pharaoh to gain Israel's freedom. Here again, each possessed something that the other didn't. God engages groups of individuals to do God's work.

While God can indeed work through people who are not a part of the church, the church is uniquely situated—and called—to bear the good news of life and liberation to a needy world. Within any given congregation people with unique gifts and capabilities can be found: business executives, bankers, attorneys, teachers, doctors, nurses, homemakers, factory workers, farmers. The list is extensive. One of the tasks of the church is to align people's gifts with other people's needs.

Identify the needs of your community. Are there homeless people? Are there tutoring or mentoring programs that need volunteers? Are there food banks that need help procuring food? Are there programs like Meals on Wheels that require drivers? No one congregation can respond to every need, but every congregation can respond to at least one need. The church and its leadership are in a position to help people in the congregation discern their gifts, their callings, and connect them with avenues of service.

One of the challenges before those of us in the church is a willingness to embrace and value the gifts that others bring to the table. This may mean being open to nontraditional ways of going about things. For one example, should we—and if so, how should we—make use of modern technology in the church? From how we go about worship, to how we communicate with the world beyond the sanctuary, technology challenges the tradition of being the church. Yet for millennials and subsequent generations, it's as much a part of their lives as books became for previous generations in the wake of Gutenberg's printing press.

Negotiating the tensions that can arise between the familiar and the new can lead to conflict. Even Moses and Aaron came into conflict with one another (cf. Exodus 32!). Still, the God who has engaged us beckons the church forward to be an engaging community on behalf of life and liberation for the larger world.

For Reflection and Action

1. Can you identify people who, by merely going about their normal lives, have made considerable contributions to the well-being of your church or community? Would you describe such instances as providential or pure chance?

2. Where are some of the places in your congregation that people are invited to share their gifts and talents?

3. How does your congregation seek to identify and develop the gifts and skills of people?

4. Take photographs of people or events in which you see people acting differently from the perception others have of them. Look for ways in which God might be working through people you know.

Law, or torah (instruction), is a gift that helps sustain the well-being of the individual and community.

Chapter 4

God Sustains

Scripture
Exodus 19:9–20:20 God sets boundaries for the people through the gift of torah.

Prayer
Sustaining God, we thank you that you not only call us but that you also nourish us throughout our journey of faith. Like rain on newly sown seeds, you water our lives with gifts that help us to grow and flourish. Word, water, and table; communities of faith, pastors, and teachers inspire and motivate us; they guide us along the paths that you place in front of us. And of course, there is your Spirit that blows through our lives, filling us with daring imagination and vision. Thank you so very much, sustaining God. Amen.

Introduction
God listens, God responds, God engages human agents, and God sustains. In the minds of most people, the word *sustenance* conjures up images of food and drink. More broadly, sustenance refers to all things necessary for the well-being of life and health. That includes food and drink, medical care, dependable social structures in family and society, leadership, productive work, rest, and even recreation. All forms of sustenance make healthy and wholesome lives possible.

For generations, Israel had lived in Egypt. To the degree that the social unit signified by the name Israel resembled or stood apart from the larger society of Egypt is impossible to say. Nevertheless, the Israelites' social identity would surely have been shaped in ways seen and unseen by the dominant Egyptian culture. When the king "who did not know Joseph" (Exodus 1:8) assumed control of Egypt, Israel's identity was brutally and forcefully molded into that of an enslaved people.

All of this would change, of course, when God's covenant people emerged safely from the sea (Exodus 14). The commanding presence of Pharaoh that had been so much a part of their lives was gone. Gone too was a settled existence, no matter how miserable it might have been. The structures and patterns that had ordered their lives for so long were no more. Everything had changed.

One thinks of a wide-eyed college freshman filled with wonder and fear hundreds of miles away from all that had been familiar for so long. The dorm room has been put in order; the family has said all good-byes; everything is new; and the possibilities seem endless. Israel must have felt something of this as the people turned their backs to the sea and headed toward Sinai. After that, who knows where? But at Sinai, the people would find sustenance that would guide them through the wilderness and through the generations to come. There they would receive torah.

A Basic Theme: God Sustains

Much of the larger Exodus story could be placed under the umbrella-like theme of "God Sustains." All of God's dealings with Israel to preserve the people's lives and growth can be viewed as sustaining deeds. What follows, though, will narrow the focus and concentrate on God's fundamental gift of law.

To many Christian ears the expression "gift of law" may sound strange. The familiar contrasts between grace and law, or faith and works, come immediately to mind. Grace and faith are viewed positively; law and works, negatively. But such a division would have been neither automatic nor straightforward for Israel. Two things to note:

> *The word typically translated as* law *in English Bibles is* torah. The word means much more than simply "law" and is better

translated as "instruction." So it is that Genesis, the first book in the first section of the Old Testament (the Torah) has almost no law as such but is mostly story. However, the story instructs in many matters.

The more pure forms of law that we encounter in the Old Testament come to us in the middle of the narrative, or, story.[1] Law is embedded in the fabric of lived experience and is intended to serve the well-being of God's covenant people. It is life giving and life sustaining.

At the heart of the Torah stand the Ten Commandments, or Decalogue (Exodus 20:1–17; cf., Deuteronomy 5). The commandments appear in the middle of a theophany, or appearance of God (Exodus 19:16—20:20). After acts of purification, the people are gathered at the foot of Mt. Sinai and can overhear the conversation between Moses and God (19:9, 19). The first words heard in this fearful exchange is God's same self-identification that Moses heard before embarking upon his mission: "I am YHWH" (20:1; cf., 3:15; 6:2). The voice does not issue the divine command before uttering words of assurance, reminding the terrified people that this God, YHWH, brought Israel out. The story of liberation precedes divine instruction.

The commandments are absolute in nature and do not make use of the conditional "if-then" form of many legal codes. All but the fourth and fifth commandments are negative: "You shall not." As such, they stake out necessary boundaries of life and make no effort to tell the people everything that they must do.

The first four commandments pertain to proper relations with God, which must surely have been good news to people terrified by God's appearance. The last six commandments concern the kinds of actions that would be harmful to family cohesion and the well-being of the broader community.

The commandments provided guidance and structure to Israel as they struggled to live with both God and one another. They were God's good gift to sustain the covenant community.

---

1. Terence E. Fretheim makes the point splendidly in *Exodus*, Interpretation: A Bible Commentary for Teaching and Preaching (Louisville, KY: Westminster John Knox Press, 1991), 201–7.

The Life of Faith: Torah as a Blessing

Even if we grant that Israel understood torah as a blessing and not a burden, is there any sense in which Christians today may make a similar claim? A brief look at two commandments would suggest that the answer to that question is "yes."

The Second Commandment prohibits the making of an image. The word *image* (Hebrew, *pesel*) refers to a statue-like image made of materials such as clay, metal, stone, or wood. Whether the image would be an effort to represent YHWH or another deity is not certain. What is certain is that any image provokes the jealousy and anger of God.

The prohibition against images would have been stunning in the ancient world. Images of various sorts were noteworthy features of most religions. How did Israel respond to such a glaring vacuum? Israel turned to poetry, or word images. The rich verbal imagery of the theophany that surrounds the Decalogue is one example (cf. Judges 5:4–5; Psalm 18:7–15). The eloquent depictions of God as the Creator in Psalm 104:1–4 or the God who comes to the exiles in Ezekiel 1 fill the void left by imageless worship. Poetic imagination replaces images.

The Second Commandment offers an invitation for people of faith to engage our creative imaginations in study, prayer, and praise. Be attentive to the rich metaphors and literary images of God when reading the Bible. Create new poetry, hymns, and music that direct our attention to God in vibrant and exciting ways. In our prayers, both private and public, step outside of familiar and formulaic speech. The bold and textured proclamation can only help us to be better bearers of the image of God.

The Fifth Commandment calls the people to honor their fathers and mothers. With the Fifth Commandment, we move from the laws that pertain to relations with God to those that instruct about matters of human interactions. Strictly speaking, the two tablets (as they are sometimes called) are not divorced from one another. Our relationships with one another intersect our relationships with God.

Children are instructed to honor (Hebrew, *kabod*) their parents, but the command does not prescribe a list of actions to be followed. The Hebrew word can carry the nuances of "respect" or "to treat with dignity." While the commandment can address younger children's relations to parents, it is quite likely here aimed at grown children who have elderly parents. Parents who are no longer able to work and contribute economically to the family, and who may, in fact, be a drain on family resources, are to be honored, respected, and treated with dignity.

In our world, it is not uncommon for children and parents to be separated by hundreds of miles. Neglect of parents is all too easy. In other cases, we frequently hear about elder abuse by family members or other caregivers. For people of faith, the call for creative insights on how to obey the Fifth Commandment is great and urgent.

The Church: Saved from Striving

The Fourth Commandment. One of the greatest gifts that helps sustain the community of faith is the gift of Sabbath. The Fourth Commandment is the last of the commandments that specifically deal with human relations to God. However, it can also be argued that it has much to say about how people relate to one another.

"Remember the Sabbath day, and keep it holy" (Exodus 20:8). On this day all work ceases for the entire community, including service animals and servants. God rested on the seventh day of creation, so Sabbath rest is built into the fabric of creation. Failure to rest on the Sabbath, then, nudges the creation back toward primordial chaos. Sabbath rest establishes a unity among people, creatures, and the earth itself.

Life can so easily be dominated by pursuits—work or play. Vocation is transformed into toil. Our fellows become competitors whom we seek to outmaneuver. A certain viciousness and bitterness loom over life until life itself is crushed. Sabbath offers the church a different vision for reality, a vision where striving ceases and stability ensues.

We need not return to the so-called "blue laws" of decades ago to keep Sabbath rest. There are many ways short of that to take time out from life and consider, as a community, our Creator. Sabbath also beckons us to find ways to advocate vocations for all people in which they can find hope and sustenance.

The Tenth Commandment. Stated negatively, the Tenth Commandment concludes the tablet that pertains to human interactions: "You shall not covet . . ." (Exodus 20:17). The Hebrew word for *covet* has the nuance of "to desire," even to the point of trying to acquire. As such, this commandment is a fitting capstone for much that has preceded, since it names the very thing that can lead to the violation of other commandments: desire. As Hosea writes, "swearing, lying, murder, stealing, and adultery . . ." (Hosea 4:2) can all erupt from unwholesome desire.

The Tenth Commandment invites people of the church to ask the questions "How is it that we go about acquiring what we acquire?" and "When is enough, enough?" While these questions can be vexing (and also more than a bit uncomfortable!), the prophets thought deeply about such matters. Amos speaks of people who can hardly wait until the end of religious festivals so that they can get about their business of fleecing the sheep (Amos 8:4–6). Micah speaks of influential people who lie awake at night designing plans to seize the possessions of the poor (Micah 2:1–22). The desire to acquire at all costs (in defiance of Sabbath observance!) leads to enslavement. Such a life is unsustainable. The church is in a unique position to consider how we can go about a sustainable life unencumbered by desire. God's torah is a gift to help just that consideration.

For Reflection and Action
1. Can you name ways that laws help sustain life? Are there some laws that do not sustain but harm instead? How should we respond to harmful laws?

2. How vital is Sabbath rest in your life? Many people pack their jobs around with them in the form of their smartphones. What are ways that we can resist the temptation to be continuously engaged by work?

3. The desire to have things can be strong indeed. Identify ways that coveting, or ardent desire, can be detrimental to the well-being of the church and community. What are some ways to avoid coveting?

4. Write each commandment and one positive thing each commandment might mean on pieces of paper. Put the paper into balloons before they are blown up. Spread the balloons around the church, give them to other groups, or distribute them in some other way.

The Bible acknowledges that God can be immediately present but is not limited to any one place.

Chapter 5

God Is Present

Scripture
Exodus 25:1–8 God gives plans for adorning the dwelling.

Exodus 33:12–16 Moses pleads with God.

Exodus 36:8–38 Workers construct the tabernacle.

Exodus 40:34–38 God's presence fills the tabernacle.

Prayer
God of cloud, fire, and tabernacle, shine forth on our lives. Sometimes the demands of life stretch before us like an unending wilderness. Deadlines at work and school, meetings without end, bills to pay, homes to keep up, and families with needs all converge and threaten to consume us. We race from task to task, running about like lost children. Help us to slow down and discern that we are not alone in a frenzied world. Open our eyes and all of our senses so that we may see your guiding presence among us and follow you as you lead us. Amen.

Introduction
The writer of Exodus is deeply concerned about God's presence. Indeed, this is a matter of considerable concern for the bulk of the whole Old Testament. However, neither Exodus nor the rest of the Old Testament offers an exhaustive, systematic pronouncement

about the presence of God. Instead, the Bible provides many differently nuanced episodes that comment on divine presence. Abraham experiences God in a visit by three mysterious strangers (Genesis 18). Jacob encounters God in a nocturnal wrestling match (Genesis 32). Moses discerns the Holy One in a burning bush (Exodus 3). And so it goes. Each encounter offers different angles of vision on what it means to talk about the presence of God. Taken together and along with the near innumerable episodes that depict divine presence, they affirm God's presence.

In the ancient world where Israel was born, the gods were strictly related to turf. To put it in another way, deities were territorial. When travelers crossed a territorial boundary, they entered the jurisdiction of a different deity and, at the same time, left the domain of the previous deity. One god's power ran out, and another god's power took over at territorial boundaries.

For the most part, Israel's understanding of divine presence seems to be different. To be sure, there were places where God's presence was especially available: Bethel, Mt. Sinai, and eventually Mt. Zion in Jerusalem, to name a few. But for Israel, the divine presence was not understood to be restricted to the land of the promise. Later, prophets (especially Isaiah) will portray YHWH as involved in the affairs of other nations. Still, God's presence was especially available for Israel.

That said, the specter of Mt. Sinai looms large, not only in Exodus but through Numbers 10:10. There the presence of God is palpably real in the clouds, smoke, lightning, and booming thunder. To be sure, the extended absence of Moses leads the people to wonder (Exodus 32). But the Holy One quickly reminds the people that God is present at Sinai.

A Basic Theme: God Tabernacles with the People
The book of Exodus is composed of three segments:
- Chapters 1–15, the liberation from Egypt and the Red Sea crossing
- Chapters 16–24, the journey to Sinai and the sealing of the covenant
- Chapters 25–40, the building of the tabernacle, filled with the glory of God

The movement from bondage to Mt. Sinai demonstrates that the ultimate goal for Israel's release is fellowship with God, being in God's presence. However, the presence of God at Mt. Sinai is both a problem and a promise for the people as they begin their journey to the land of promise. The problem is twofold:

Will God stay? The commanding presence of God so closely associated with Sinai might lead the Israelites to wonder if the two are inseparably connected. However, Mt. Sinai is not Israel's final destination. When the time is right, the people will break camp and leave Sinai to begin their journey toward the land of the promise. Thus, they might have reasoned, the further they travel from the mountain, the further they are from God.

Will God go? The golden calf incident raises the question of how the awesome holiness of God can accompany a people who are given to idolatry. The question lingers—"Will God go?" In a dramatic encounter Moses daringly negotiates an answer to this question (33:1-6, 12-23). Here, God has said, "'I will not go up among you, or I would consume you on the way'" (33:3). Moses boldly reminds God that the people, disobedient though they may be, are still God's people (33:12-13). God, in turn, pledges that the divine presence will indeed journey with the people.

The tabernacle provides the means whereby God may safely dwell and move with the people on their journey. Nearly a third of Exodus is devoted to the tabernacle. First come instructions for building the tabernacle and its contents (25:1–31:11), and later the tabernacle is constructed (35:4–40:33). The golden calf incident stands between the instructions and the construction. The design of the tabernacle closely resembles the subsequent temple. Indeed, the temple likely influenced the Exodus description of the tabernacle. Notable differences between the two were that the tabernacle was an elaborate portable tent while the temple was stone and wood and fixed. Each provided a place where God could "dwell" safely among the people (25:8).

Actually, two tent traditions in Exodus sometimes seem to be fused together. Exodus 25–31 speaks of a tabernacle (*mishkan*), related to the Hebrew verb that means "to dwell." Further, the tabernacle is situated in the midst of the people (Exodus 25:8). Here, God may descend from the heavenly temple and safely dwell in the middle of the camp. The tent tradition reflected in Exodus 33:7–11 speaks of a "tent of meeting" situated outside of the camp where God descends to meet periodically with Moses. Each tradition speaks of the divine presence, but differently.

The promise? If the people can learn to live faithfully in the presence of a Holy God, there just may be a way through the wilderness, and there just may be a land "flowing with milk and honey" on the other side.

The Life of Faith: A Tabernacle Journey

It is not likely that any of us live our lives in the shadow of a tabernacle. More than likely, the very notion of a "tent of many colors" filled with strange religious objects seems quite odd. So how might this "tent story" intersect with our own personal stories on our own journeys of faith?

As people of faith, we find ourselves surrounded by an increasingly secular and unholy world. The question sometimes heard— "Isn't anything sacred anymore?"—is to the point. In such a world, religious imagination withers. It is difficult to discern—or even believe—that God is at work among us. Many of us, perhaps unwittingly, are inclined to join in with the people at the foot of Sinai waiting for Moses to come down the mountain. We cling to the golden calves of our various technologies believing that they will lead us safely into the future.

The tabernacle story is an invitation to undertake a bold act of religious imagination and affirmation. Despite appearances, God is present. The world is not the secular place, void of God, that we might think. When the Judean king Ahaz faced a hostile coalition that sought to kill him around 734 BCE, he had to be reminded that there's more to life than meets the eye. Pointing at a pregnant young woman, Isaiah said that she will give birth and name the infant Immanuel—"God is with us." All that Ahaz could see was looming death. Isaiah saw "God is with us" and life (Isaiah 7).

The realization that God is present allows us to live boldly in the present and into the future. To be sure, the presence of God does not eliminate all of the obstacles from our lives. But it does mean that when we face terrifying circumstances, we are not alone. When a child goes to school and spends the first day away from parents, that child is not alone. When the same child leaves for college years later, God is present. When the doctor, following tests, utters the chilling word "cancer," God is present. And when our beloved friend or family member is slowly taken away from us by Alzheimer's, neither that one nor we are alone. God is present.

When we step forward to challenge the injustices in the world, we are not alone. When we take bold stands on behalf of people created in God's image, God is present. When we speak out against the religious intolerance against Muslims; when we stand in solidarity against oppression and victimization of African Americans, immigrants throughout the world, and sexism that still means women doing the same jobs as men are paid less, God is present. We are not alone.

The tabernacle story reminds us that God is not merely with us but that the divine presence leads. When the presence of God, represented by the cloud, moves forward, the people follow. When it rests, they rest. The tabernacle journey is one that God leads.

The Church: Liturgy and the World

The instructions for constructing the tabernacle and the objects housed therein do not make for the most exciting reading in the Bible. Indeed, for those adventurous people who tent-camp, Exodus 25–31 may send shudders up and down the spine because of the eerie similarity to the instructions for setting up a multipiece cabin tent! All of the attention given to detail—the dimensions, materials, color—does not excite. But for the priestly minded people whose theology informs these chapters, details matter. The construction of the tabernacle is not unlike God's creation of the world. What takes place in the tabernacle contributes not just to the well-being of the people gathered around the sanctuary but also to the welfare of the world. Liturgy matters!

The attention given to detail in the construction of the tabernacle invites us to pause and think theologically about what transpires in our communities of faith when we gather on Sunday mornings. Worship planners and leaders are reminded of the urgent importance of how the various parts of the whole fit together and what they communicate about God. While worship is a vital part of leading the people of God into greater faithfulness, it is crucial to consider how worship contributes to the well-being of the larger world. Does what happens in worship stay in worship, or does it spill over into the whole of creation?

While the tabernacle, with all of its holy objects and rituals, makes it possible for God to travel safely with the people, it by no means domesticates God. The uneasy mix of a holy, mighty God and an undisciplined group of people inclined to pursue their own interests leads to a lingering sense of threat in the God-Israel relationship. The risk can be diminished but not entirely eliminated. That is the nature of the Holy.

The raw, unchained power of the Sinai God portrayed in Exodus is not the dominant view of God in most mainline churches today. The church has mostly moved on from the "hellfire and damnation" theology characteristic of days long gone, and there are more positives than negatives about this theological shift. But has the church lost something by ignoring the awesome and holy otherness of God that Exodus shines forth? Perhaps.

While the Exodus texts say little about the specific meaning of some of the tabernacle's objects, Leviticus will offer more insight (cf. Leviticus 1–7; 16). One of the functions of "tabernacle worship" is atonement. God gives the people a way of making life in the presence of the Holy possible.

The tendency in certain quarters of the church to focus on praise, even to the point of excluding any notions of confession, is bothersome. Praise can be a great Band-Aid that hides the ugliness of life—somewhat like celebrating Easter resurrection without mentioning the cross or the tomb. The holiness of God's presence in a tabernacle or church is a full-throated call to avail ourselves to the divine gifts of confession and forgiveness.

For Reflection and Action
1. Read Psalm 139 and Job 7. Each has a different take on divine presence. Is God's presence always comforting, or can it also be disturbing and frightening? How?

2. In what ways does your church's liturgy inform and shape your life? Does it become familiar, old, and dull, or does its regular rhythm structure and nurture your life? How?

3. How does your congregation acknowledge the holiness of God in both liturgy and life?

4. Develop a template to help the children in your family or church create greeting cards that give assurance of God's presence. Suggest persons or places where they can be delivered.

The God we meet in Exodus is both sensitive to the needs of the people and stern in covenant expectations.

Chapter 6

God Is Merciful and Gracious

Scripture
Exodus 34:1–9 God offers a deep look into the divine character.

Prayer
Great God, your awesome holiness is exceeded only by your mercy and grace. So many times we have failed to live up to your covenant expectations. We have turned our backs on you and trusted instead in our own ingenuity to secure our lives on our own. We have neglected your guiding presence and set out on our own paths, only to fall flat on our faces. Yet you have not forsaken us and left us to our own devices. You have picked us up and set us back on right paths, and for that we give you thanks and praise. Amen.

Introduction
The God we meet in Exodus is a complex God, perhaps even inscrutable. God seems to have been only remotely concerned about the plight of Israel until the people cried out (Exodus 2:24). To be sure, two midwives violated Pharaoh's command to kill the newborn male babies, and Israel multiplied. But God jumps into high gear only after the people's outcry. Then, after God selects Moses to be a principal agent in liberating Israel, God suddenly appears, seeking to kill Moses on his mission to obey God (4:24–26)! Pharaoh is the

primary obstacle to Israel's departure from Egypt, yet God chooses to make Pharaoh ever more resolute in his refusal to free Israel (for example, 7:3; 9:12; 10:20). Strange indeed! So what do we make of this mysterious and complicated mountain God? The question can only be answered as the larger story of the exodus unfolds.

Exodus 34:1-9 is a crucial text for understanding the God of the exodus. Indeed, as will be discussed below, it is an exceedingly important text that occurs in various forms throughout the Old Testament. Curiously, the first utterance of this bold affirmation about God's character—the Lord is merciful and gracious—follows closely the people's provocation of God by fashioning a golden calf (Exodus 32). That deed elicits both God's and Moses' wrath (32:7-10, 15-20) and results in Moses' destruction of the first copy of the Ten Commandments. Only after Exodus 34:1-9 are the commandments rewritten. As such, the amazing utterance by God about the Divine Self stands between past infidelity and future possibility, broken commandments and fresh instructions. Two of the basic claims made by the proclamation of Exodus 34:6-7 (that God is merciful and gracious but also holds wrongdoers accountable) are appropriately framed by the fiery destruction of the original tablets and God's gracious gift of a new set of tablets. The mysterious complexity of the Exodus God, then, lies between the two pillars of divine righteous indignation and divine compassion. Such is the textured depth of the Exodus God, and the God we serve.

A Basic Theme: God Is Merciful and Gracious

The divine pronouncement in Exodus 34:6-7 begins with a double utterance of the name YHWH ("the LORD"). This is not the first time that the Lord has spoken the divine name in Exodus. One has to return to 3:15 where God introduces the Divine Self to Moses from the burning bush. There the name YHWH is linked to the Hebrew verb "to be" in a phrase that is traditionally translated "I am who I am" (3:14) but likely is better rendered "I will be who I will be." In other words, in Exodus 3 the reader must wait to find out who the Lord will be, much like Moses must wait to find out. By Exodus 34, we have seen God act to liberate the oppressed covenant people (Exodus 3-14) and also to exercise stern judgment (Exodus 32:30-34). The reader has been shown both the mercy and the judgment of God between chapters 3 and 34. Now the reader is told the nature of God (Exodus 34:6–7) explicitly.

Exodus 34:6–7 is confessional, or creedal, in nature. Such statements represent an effort by the faithful to gather up and summarize basic discernments about God that come through a lived history in a relationship with God. They are not initially propositional or "thesis" statements made at the beginning of a logical argument. However, once formulated, creeds and confessional statements can become a beginning point and reaffirm guidance for generations who follow in the wake of the creed's origination. So creeds and confessions arise from the life of faith, and they give birth to new lives of faith.

This text, or clear allusions to it, is repeated in numerous places in the Old Testament (for example, Numbers 14:18; Nehemiah 8:17; Psalms 103:8–14; 145:8; Jonah 4:2, to name a few). It is also suggestive that in Nehemiah, the Psalms, and Jonah there are no references to "visiting sins upon children." As such, these traditions seem intentionally to stress the compassion and mercy of the Lord.

God's merciful and gracious character imbues the text with a comforting and assuring tone—especially in the wake of Exodus 32. That God should saddle four generations of descendants with the failings of the parents seems harsh. There are at least two ways to understand the inclusion of multiple generations in divine punishment. One would be *linear*, which would measure the duration of the sentence over an extended number of years. Another way would be *synchronic*, which would involve an extended family living as a single household at a given moment. In either case, the notion that children would suffer for the failings of their parents is bothersome. Still, the punishment extends only four generations while God's mercy, grace, steadfast love, and loyalty span thousands of years. Ultimately God's mercy and grace far outstrip divine judgment! Lack of fidelity to God has consequences, but the kindness and compassion that reside in the heart of God prevail, even in the midst of human failure.

The Life of Faith: Bounded by Mercy and Accountability

While the awesome holiness of the Sinai God is a reality to be reckoned with seriously, the good news of Exodus 34 is that the character of God is stacked on the side of mercy. What might this mean for the life of faith?

At the end of the day, many of us are looking for some compassion because the world around us demonstrates so little of it. We know the script all too well. Bitter partisan politics and the complete loss of civil discourse that in turn result in the dehumanizing and demonizing of those who disagree with us are the norms. Walls are built on the southern border to keep people out, and when they fail, as walls always do, immigrants are detained; parents and children, husbands and wives are separated and imprisoned. Some people look on and cheer; others see and weep. White supremacists and nationalistic movements rally while mass murderers kill. Mercy and compassion seem to have disappeared along with civil discourse.

In all of this chaos and discord, in our moments of most profound consternation, we can be assured that we are still embraced and wrapped in the mercy of God. As the poet of Psalm 139 puts it, the presence of God—and in this case, the merciful presence of God—surrounds us wherever we may find ourselves and in whatever circumstances we may face. This is good news!

In Deuteronomy's version of the Ten Commandments, the rationale for Sabbath rest is different from the reasoning in Exodus 20:8–11, which grounds Sabbath rest in God's rest on the seventh day. Deuteronomy anchors Sabbath rest in God's act of liberating Israel from slavery and hard toil (5:12–15). Israel is instructed to provide a time of rest for everyone and everything in the household. A liberated people become a liberating people. In the same manner, to be recipients of divine mercy and compassion is also a call to be merciful and compassionate people to all around us. Exodus 34:1–9 is also a vocational summons. A life of faith is a life that searches out ways to convey mercy and compassion to a world so badly in need of them.

We cannot forget that our actions have consequences that affect other people and, indeed, the larger world around us (cf. Hosea 4:1–3). To succumb to and purvey bitterness and hatred, in turn, bring them back on our own heads and the heads of others. There can be little doubt that our own actions can affect subsequent generations. An abused child, a child separated from parents, or a child with parents addicted to opioids or alcohol can be scarred for life. To be recipients of divine mercy and compassion calls for us to be bearers of the image of a merciful and gracious God. This is perhaps the most essential vocation of all.

The Church: A Community Bounded by Mercy and Accountability

No less than individuals struggling to live a life of faith, the church as a community of God's people is also bounded by divine mercy and accountability. Seven expressions in Exodus 34:6–7a enumerate God's benevolent characteristics: "merciful," "gracious," "slow to anger," "abounding in steadfast love and faithfulness," "keeping steadfast love," and "forgiving iniquity." The collective force of these expressions is considerable, and the significance of each expression on its own is powerful. Two are singled out here for consideration:

> *Merciful.* The Hebrew word that is translated as "merciful" is related to the Hebrew word for "womb." Old Testament scholar Phyllis Trible has convincingly argued that the word for "mercy" suggests the kind of compassion that a mother feels for the unborn child in her womb.[1] Such is the stance of God toward Israel and, by extension, the church.

> *Steadfast love.* The word translated as "steadfast love," repeated twice here, is especially descriptive of the relationship between partners bound in covenant. Here it expresses God's deep resolve to maintain the covenantal tie with Israel (and the church). In fact, it was God's remembering of, and steadfastness to, the covenant with the ancestors that helped launch the entire Exodus story (2:24).

In a time when church institutions seem assailed by financial woes that threaten overseas mission work, new church development, curriculum resources, and church insurance and retirement programs; when church membership rolls are dwindling, and congregations are closing doors, it is good to remember that God's parental mercy and steadfast devotion to the church hold firm.

---

1. Phyllis Trible, *God and the Rhetoric of Sexuality*, Overtures to Biblical Theology (Philadelphia: Fortress Press, 1978), 31–59.

We are not alone in this matter of being the church. When we forget that, we are tempted to repeat the failure of the people at the foot of Sinai who sought to rescue their own existence by making their own god. Such actions inevitably diminish the church.

As with the life of faith for an individual, so also for the communal experience of faith for the church. There is mercy, and there is accountability. Perhaps this is nowhere more evident than in the bold proclamation that God forgives iniquity, on the one hand, (34:7a) and the stunning acknowledgment that God "visits iniquity" on others (34:7b). The Hebrew word translated as "forgives" has the meaning of "to lift" or "to bear/carry." It is, for example, the verb used when Ruth carries an ephah (about a half bushel) of gleaned barley back to her home (Ruth 2:18). But God can just as easily place this burden on successive generations of one who violates covenant stipulations. As Walter Brueggemann has seen perhaps better than anyone, there is an irresolvable tension in the character of God.[2] A covenant life entails special accountability. While God's benevolence outstrips God's judgment seven to two, the church that receives mercy is also held accountable to the covenant-keeping God.

For Reflection and Action

1. Does your congregation make use of creeds or confessions (for example, the Apostles' Creed)? If so, how do they help shape your life?

2. Name the places around your congregation where mercy and compassion seem most to be lacking. Are there specific ways that you or your congregation can respond to this lack?

3. Can you name ways that you have experienced mercy, either from God or other people? How did you react? Does being accountable to God insist that we share what we have received?

---

2. Walter Brueggemann, "The Book of Exodus," in *New Interpreters' Bible* (Nashville: Abingdon, 1994), 947, 951.

4. Write a song or poem thanking God for forgiving you when you have wronged someone or have wronged God.

Group Gatherings

Eva Stimson

Group Gathering 1

God Listens

Main Idea
Not only does God speak and act, but God also listens. Because being heard can be liberating and healing, the church is called to follow the example of God in Exodus and become a listening community.

Preparing to Lead
- Read and reflect on chapter 1, "God Listens."
- Review this plan for the group gathering, and select questions and activities that you will use.
- Gather newsprint and markers, if needed, and prepare to post newsprint sheets on a wall or bulletin board.
- What other questions, issues, or themes occur to you from your reflection?

Gathering
- Provide name tags and pens as people arrive.
- Provide simple refreshments; ask volunteers to bring refreshments for the next five gatherings.
- Agree on simple ground rules and organization (for example, time to begin and end; location for gatherings; welcoming of all points of view; confidentiality; and so on). Encourage participants to bring their study books and Bibles.
- Have available paper and pens or pencils.
- Review the gathering format: Gathering, Opening Worship, Conversation, and Conclusion.

Opening Worship
Prayer (unison)
Sometimes, God, it seems as if there are so many words—too many. Everyone is talking, and no one really bothers to listen.

Sometimes it feels like what we have to say, yearn to speak, or need to say gets squeezed out because of so many words. But you have shown yourself, again and again, to be a listening God who hears our outcries—even welcomes them. And more, we have found healing in your listening, and we thank you. Help us to become engaged listeners too, and perhaps as we listen to others, we may become agents of healing. Amen.

Prayerful, Reflective Reading
- Read Exodus 33:7–11 aloud.
- Invite all to reflect for a few minutes in silence.
- After reflection time, invite all to listen for a word or phrase as the passage is reread and to reflect on that word or phrase in silence.
- Read the passage a third time, asking all to offer a silent prayer following the reading.
- Invite volunteers to share the word or phrase that spoke most deeply to them.

Prayer
Loving God, hear our prayers today as we seek to follow you more faithfully:

(*spoken prayers may be offered*)

Hear us now as we pray together, saying, Our Father . . .

Conversation
- Introduce chapter 1, "God Listens." Share observations, reflections, and insights.
- Review the Introduction (pp. 1–2). Share these key points:
  a. The opening of Exodus reminds us of God's promise to Abraham, Isaac, and Jacob in Genesis.
  b. The story of Exodus sets into motion events that will eventually bring together the twin pillars of God's promise to the ancestors: land and descendants.
  c. The first major section of Exodus has an almost lament-like structure: outcry, petitions along the way, and finally affirmation with thanksgiving.
- Review "A Basic Theme: God Listens" (pp. 2–4). Distribute paper and pens or pencils. Have participants write in a few

sentences what they would say if someone asked, "What do you believe about God?" Have them review what they have written and circle references to God's actions. Then have them underline references to God's words. Ask:

Did anyone mention God's listening?

Divide a sheet of newsprint into three columns with the headings "God acts," "God speaks," and "God listens." Invite participants to give any examples they can think of from the Old Testament, especially Exodus, of God acting, speaking, and listening. List these in the appropriate column, noting which list is the longest. Ask:

Which of the three do you tend to emphasize in your own view of God?

Why do you think God's words and actions often tend to be noticed more than God's listening?

Form two groups to look more closely at examples of God's listening. Have one group read Exodus 15:22-25; 16:1-17:7; the other group reads Exodus 32:1-14, noting what gets God's attention (complaints, petition, intercession) and how God listens and responds. Have someone from each group report on the discussion.

- Review "The Life of Faith: God Listens to Us" (pp. 4-5). Share these key points:
  a. Listening is a mark of the fundamental character of God.
  b. The God who heard the outcry of oppressed slaves in the past is the same God who hears us today and responds in our times of need.
  c. God is accessible and dependable in a world where genuine dialogue and conversation are all too rare.

Read aloud Psalm 13. Ask:

Where does the tone shift in this lament (i.e., between verses 4 and 5)?

What might account for the radical change? Could it be the result of having been heard by God?

- Review "The Church: A Listening Community" (pp. 5–6). Have participants reflect silently on the first question in For Reflection and Action (p. 6). Suggest that they reread Exodus 33:7–11 and imagine themselves bringing a need or petition into the tent of meeting. Ask: How does it feel to be heard by God? By other members of your community of faith? What happens when people are not heard and keep issues bottled up inside of them?

  Form several groups, and discuss the second and third questions in For Reflection and Action (p. 6). Have someone in each group record ideas about how the church can become a listening, healing community for people in need. Have each group share its thoughts.

Conclusion
Invite participants to lift up prayers for people or groups in your community who cry out to be heard. Thank God for listening.

Passing the Peace
The peace of Christ be with you.
    And also with you.
Amen.

Group Gathering 2

God Responds

Main Idea
God listens and responds as both covenant keeper and Creator, acting for the sake of God's covenant people and for the sake of the world. Like the Israelites at the edge of the sea, the church today is challenged to "stand firm" in faithfulness to God while remaining open to the wind of the spirit—the new work God is doing.

Preparing to Lead
- Read and reflect on chapter 2, "God Responds."
- Review this plan for the group gathering, and select questions and activities that you will use.
- Gather newsprint and markers, if needed, and prepare to post newsprint sheets on a wall or bulletin board.
- What other questions, issues, or themes occur to you from your reflection?

Gathering
- Provide simple refreshments as people arrive and name tags if still needed.

Opening Worship
Prayer (unison)
Gracious Lord, you have pledged to be our God and have called us to be your people. Bound to you in covenant, we are bold to call out to you in praise and in need. We are thankful that you not only hear our prayers but that you have both the power and inclination to respond. You have brought us through deep waters in the past, and we trust your guidance now and in the future. When our backs are against the wall, and all seems lost, your sure and certain help sees us through. We give you thanks. Amen.

Prayerful, Reflective Reading
- Read Exodus 6:1–9 aloud.
- Invite all to reflect for a few minutes in silence.
- After reflection time, invite all to listen for a word or phrase as the passage is reread and to reflect on that word or phrase in silence.
- Read the passage a third time, asking all to offer a silent prayer following the reading.
- Invite volunteers to share the word or phrase that spoke most deeply to them.

Prayer
Loving God, hear our prayers today as we seek to follow you more faithfully:

(spoken prayers may be offered)

Hear us now as we pray together, saying, Our Father . . .

Conversation
- Introduce chapter 2, "God Responds." Share observations, reflections, and insights.
- Review the Introduction (pp. 7–8). Share these key points:
  a. God is covenant keeper. God responds because of the covenant made with Abraham, Isaac, and Jacob (God's people).
  b. God also responds as the Creator, a theme that runs through Exodus as well as Genesis.
  c. As covenant keeper and Creator, God acts both for the sake of Israel and for the sake of the world.
- Review "A Basic Theme: God Responds" (pp. 8–10). Have someone read aloud the account of God's establishing a covenant with Abraham in Genesis 12:1–2. Note how God reminds Moses of this covenant in Exodus 6. Skim through the first ten chapters of Exodus, noting the many references to "my people." Recall the story of the golden calf from Exodus 32. Ask:

  How does this incident affect the covenant relationship between God and Israel? How does God respond?

- Review "The Life of Faith: Living in Covenant with the Creator" (pp. 10–11). On a sheet of newsprint write "covenant" and "contract." Ask:

    Is there any difference between a covenant and a contract? If so, what are the differences? (For example, a covenant implies permanence and commitment.)

    What are some examples of covenant relationships? (For example, marriages, promises made at baptism by the child's parents and congregation.)

    What does it mean to be in a covenant relationship with God?

    Form several groups to discuss the questions in For Reflection and Action (pp. 12–13). Have someone from each group share highlights of the discussion.
    Have someone read aloud Isaiah 40:21–31. Spend a few minutes reflecting silently on what it means to be in covenant relationship with the Creator.
- Review "The Church: God's People" (pp. 11–12). Post two or three sheets of newsprint lengthwise, and make a timeline of events in Exodus 3–14: God calls Moses in the burning bush (Exodus 3); Moses' first unsuccessful attempt to free the slaves (4); God reminds Moses of the covenant (6); the plagues—a contest between God and Pharaoh (7–12); the Passover and flight from Egypt (12–13); crossing the Red Sea (14). Ask:

    What does Moses tell the people to do in Exodus 14:13?

    What does God tell Moses to do in verses 15–16?

    What does God do in verse 21?

    Is there a message here for the church?

    Form several groups. Have each group read the final paragraph of chapter 2 and discuss what it might mean for your congregation to stand firm in faith while remaining open to the new work of God's spirit. Have someone from each group share highlights of the discussion.

Conclusion
Invite participants to pray for the strength to stand firm while being open to the spirit.

Passing the Peace
The peace of Christ be with you.
    And also with you.
Amen.

Group Gathering 3

God Engages Human Agents

Main Idea
When ordinary people step forward in faith to meet a need, God can transform regular, mundane work into a life-saving vocation. God engages groups (the church) to do things that cannot be done by one person alone.

Preparing to Lead
- Read and reflect on chapter 3, "God Engages Human Agents."
- Review this plan for the group gathering, and select questions and activities that you will use.
- Gather newsprint and markers, if needed, and prepare to post newsprint sheets on a wall or bulletin board.
- What other questions, issues, or themes occur to you from your reflection?

Gathering
- Provide simple refreshments as people arrive and name tags if still needed.

Opening Worship
Prayer (unison)
Thank you, God, for gifts and the opportunities to use them. You have endowed each of us with unique talents, abilities, and vision, and you beckon us to use them for the well-being of all your people, all your world. We confess that sometimes we fail to use our gifts wisely. At other times we are timid and hesitant even to attempt to use them. But you have called us and have promised to be with us through our successes and our failures. Embolden and empower us to be your faithful agents in a very needy world. Amen.

Prayerful, Reflective Reading
- Read Exodus 3:1–12 aloud.
- Invite all to reflect for a few minutes in silence.
- After reflection time, invite all to listen for a word or phrase as the passage is reread and to reflect on that word or phrase in silence.
- Read the passage a third time, asking all to offer a silent prayer following the reading.
- Invite volunteers to share the word or phrase that spoke most deeply to them.

Prayer
Loving God, hear our prayers today as we seek to follow you more faithfully:

(spoken prayers may be offered)

Hear us now as we pray together, saying, Our Father . . .

Conversation
- Introduce chapter 3, "God Engages Human Agents." Share observations, reflections, and insights.
- Invite participants to spend one minute (keep time) thinking of a person or persons who have had a significant effect on their lives. Ask those who are willing to share a bit about the people who came to mind and why they were so significant.
- Review the Introduction (pp. 15–16). Share these key points:
  a. The Bible does not speak of God in an abstract or purely philosophical fashion but tells stories of the Holy One interacting with the world and its creatures.
  b. The God we encounter in the Bible is more than capable of acting without human assistance but also chooses to involve human agents.
  c. God has made humans with creative leadership capacities so that they can act in ways that support God's creational desire without being directly instructed or can act as a result of the divine call.
- Review "A Basic Theme: God Engages Human Agents" (pp. 16–18). Divide participants into two groups. Have one group read Exodus 1:15–2:10. Have the other group read Exodus

4:10; 6:28–9:13, recalling their prayerful reflection earlier on Exodus 3:1–12. Have them list the human agents in the passages, noting which characters are named and the actions of each. Have the groups share their lists. Ask:

Why is it significant that the midwives are named? Why do you think Pharaoh's name is never given?

How does God engage humans in these stories in accomplishing divine purposes? Do you think these actions are guided by providence or chance?

Form several groups and discuss the first question in For Reflection and Action (pp. 20–21).
- Review "The Life of Faith: Vocations for All" (pp. 18–19). On a sheet of newsprint, write "Vocation." Ask:

    How would you define "vocation"?

    What is the difference between work and vocation?

Write ideas on the newsprint. Have participants return to their two groups and look again at the passages read earlier for examples of how everyday work can be transformed into a life-saving vocation. Ask:

What are the five women in Exodus 1 and 2 doing when we first meet them? How did their actions become extraordinary?

What was Moses' work in Exodus 3? What did God call him to do?

Have someone from each group report on the discussion. Have participants reflect silently on their vocation or calling.
- Review "The Church: Engaged and Engaging" (pp. 19–20). Form several groups, and discuss the second and third questions in For Reflection and Action (pp. 20–21). Ask also:

    What are some things that your church has done that could not have been done by a lone individual?

Group Gathering 3   59

What are some needs in your community that beg for common responses?

Have someone from each group report on the discussion.

Conclusion
Tell participants that the next session will consider "religious imagination" and how we use words to describe God. Invite them each to write a poem, song, or prayer that conveys something about God's nature and character as they have experienced them and bring it to your next group gathering to share if they are willing.

Passing the Peace
The peace of Christ be with you.
    And also with you.
Amen.

Group Gathering 4

God Sustains

Main Idea
Israel understood the law, or torah (instruction), as a gift that helped sustain the well-being of the individual and community. For example, the prohibition of physical images of God (or other gods) is an invitation to the religious imagination, and by keeping the Sabbath, God's people are saved from striving.

Preparing to Lead
- Read and reflect on chapter 4, "God Sustains."
- Review this plan for the group gathering, and select questions and activities that you will use.
- Gather newsprint and markers, if needed, and prepare to post newsprint sheets on a wall or bulletin board.
- What other questions, issues, or themes occur to you from your reflection?

Gathering
- Provide simple refreshments as people arrive and name tags if still needed.

Opening Worship
Prayer (unison)
Sustaining God, we thank you that you not only call us but that you also nourish us throughout our journey of faith. Like rain on newly sown seeds, you water our lives with gifts that help us to grow and flourish. The gifts of Scripture with its instruction, communities of faith, pastors, and teachers inspire and motivate us; they guide us along the paths that you place in front of us. And

of course, there is your Spirit that blows through our live, filling us with daring imagination and vision. Thank you so very much, sustaining God. Amen.

Prayerful, Reflective Reading
- Read Exodus 20:1–17 aloud.
- Invite all to reflect for a few minutes in silence.
- After reflection time, invite all to listen for a word or phrase as the passage is reread and to reflect on that word or phrase in silence.
- Read the passage a third time, asking all to offer a silent prayer following the reading.
- Invite volunteers to share the word or phrase that spoke most deeply to them.

Prayer
Loving God, hear our prayers today as we seek to follow you more faithfully:

(*spoken prayers may be offered*)

Hear us now as we pray together, saying, Our Father . . .

Conversation
- Introduce chapter 4, "God Sustains." Share observations, reflections, and insights.
- Review the Introduction (pp. 23–24). On a sheet of newsprint, write "sustain" and "sustenance." Invite participants to think of forms of sustenance that enable us to live wholesome lives (food, drink, health care, rest, meaningful work, and so forth). List these on the newsprint. Note that this session considers how God sustained the people of Israel and sustains us today.
- Review "A Basic Theme: God Sustains" (pp. 24–25). On a sheet of newsprint, write "law." Have participants stand up and move to one side of the room if their initial reaction to this word is positive and to the other side if their response is negative. If their feelings are mixed, they may stand somewhere in between. Ask:

    Why do Christians sometimes have a negative view of the law, or doing good works?

> *How can the law be a good gift from God?*
>
> *Are there bad laws, and if so do they need to be changed? How do we go about enacting changes required?*

On the same sheet of newsprint, write "torah," noting that the Hebrew word for law is better translated as "instruction." Look together at Exodus 19:9–20:20, noting the following:
a. The Ten Commandments, or Decalogue, come in the middle of the story of God's appearance to the people (theophany) following their liberation from slavery in Egypt.
b. All but two of the commandments (the fourth and fifth) are stated negatively.
c. The first four commandments pertain to proper relations with God.
d. The last six commandments concern relationships with family and community.

- Review "The Life of Faith: Torah as a Blessing" (pp. 26–27). Share these key points:
  a. The Second Commandment's prohibition against images would have been stunning in the ancient world, where images were noteworthy features of most religions.
  b. For Israel, poetic imagination replaced images.
  c. The Second Commandment offers an invitation for people of faith to engage our creative vision in study, prayer, and praise.

  Invite participants to share a poem, song, or prayer about God that they have written, and/or have someone read aloud an example of poetic imagination from the Bible, such as Judges 5:4–5; Psalm 18:7–15; or Psalm 104:1–4.

- Review "The Church: Saved from Striving" (pp. 27–28). Form three groups. Assign each group one of the following commandments: Fourth (Sabbath-keeping); Fifth (honoring parents); and Tenth (coveting). Have them review relevant material in chapter 4 and discuss:

  > *How is the commandment a gift to family/church/community?*
  >
  > *How does it help sustain our lives today?*

Suggest that the groups also discuss questions 2 and 3 in For Reflection and Action (pp. 28–29). Have each group share insights.

Conclusion
Read aloud together Psalm 104:1–4 or one of the poems or prayers written by participants.

Passing the Peace
The peace of Christ be with you.
    And also with you.
Amen.

Group Gathering 5

God Is Present

Main Idea
God is present with us but is not limited to any one place. Exodus views the tabernacle as a way that God may safely dwell among the people and at the same time be on the move. Liturgy ("work of the people") makes possible a relationship between a holy God and a not-so-holy community.

Preparing to Lead
- Read and reflect on chapter 5, "God Is Present."
- Review this plan for the group gathering, and select questions and activities that you will use.
- Gather newsprint and markers, if needed, and prepare to post newsprint sheets on a wall or bulletin board.
- Have church bulletins available. Invite your pastor, music director, or a member of the worship committee to talk about the theological rationale for the various elements in a typical worship service during your discussion of "The Church: Liturgy and the World" (pp. 35–36).
- What other questions, issues, or themes occur to you from your reflection?

Gathering
- Provide simple refreshments as people arrive and name tags if still needed.

Opening Worship
Prayer (unison)
God of cloud, fire, and tabernacle, shine forth on our lives. Sometimes the demands of life stretch before us like an unending

wilderness. Deadlines at work and school, meetings without end, bills to pay, homes to keep up, and families with needs all converge and threaten to consume us. We race from task to task running about like lost children. Help us to slow down and discern that we are not alone in a frenzied world. Open our eyes and all of our senses so that we may see your guiding presence among us and follow you as you lead us. Amen.

Prayerful, Reflective Reading
- Read Exodus 33:12–16 aloud.
- Invite all to reflect for a few minutes in silence.
- After reflection time, invite all to listen for a word or phrase as the passage is reread and to reflect on that word or phrase in silence.
- Read the passage a third time, asking all to offer a silent prayer following the reading.
- Invite volunteers to share the word or phrase that spoke most deeply to them.

Prayer
Loving God, hear our prayers today as we seek to follow you more faithfully:

(*spoken prayers may be offered*)

Hear us now as we pray together, saying, Our Father . . .

Conversation
- Introduce chapter 5, "God Is Present." Share observations, reflections, and insights.
- Review the Introduction (pp. 31–32). Share these key points:
  a. The Old Testament offers many different examples of how God is present with people.
  b. In the ancient world, deities were territorial, but Israel's understanding of divine presence was different.
  c. God's presence was especially available for Israel at Mt. Sinai and other holy places, but God was also present and involved in the affairs of other nations.
- Review "A Basic Theme: God Tabernacles with the People" (pp. 32–34). Note the references in Exodus to a "tent of meet-

ing" as well as a tabernacle—both providing a means for God to dwell safely with and travel with the people. Form several groups. Have the groups read and compare Psalm 139 and Job 7 and discuss the first question in For Reflection and Action (pp. 36–37). Ask:

How/where did the people of Israel experience God's presence?

How/where do we experience God's presence today?

When might the presence of God be a problem rather than a welcomed promise?

- Review "The Life of Faith: A Tabernacle Journey" (pp. 34–35). Spend a few minutes in silent reflection on the following (post on newsprint):

    Picture yourself in the Exodus story. Where/how do you see yourself experiencing God's presence? At the foot of Mt. Sinai? In the tabernacle or tent of meeting? Following the cloud or pillar of fire to an unknown destination?

    When/how have you experienced God's presence most vividly today?

    Where/how is God present today in places we might not expect?

    How is God leading you to take an action that may be difficult? How does it help to know that you are not alone?

    Have participants pair up and share insights.
- Review "The Church: Liturgy and the World" (pp. 35–36). Note the lengthy and detailed instructions for the tabernacle in Exodus 25–31. On a sheet of newsprint, write "Liturgy = work of the people." Ask:

    What is significant about the attention given to building the tabernacle?

    Why are the details of our worship important today? Why does liturgy matter?

Distribute church worship bulletins, and talk about the various elements in a typical worship service. Have your pastor, music director, or a member of the worship committee talk about the theological rationale for what is included and how things are ordered in the service. Form several groups, and discuss the second and third questions in For Reflection and Action (pp. 36–37). Have someone from each group report highlights of the discussion.

Conclusion
Read aloud Exodus 40:34-38. Pray a prayer of thanksgiving for God's continued presence and leading.

Passing the Peace
The peace of Christ be with you.
   And also with you.
Amen.

Group Gathering 6

God Is Merciful and Gracious

Main Idea
The God we meet in Exodus is a complex God—merciful but also expecting accountability. Lack of fidelity to God has consequences, but the mercy and compassion that reside in the heart of God prevail, even in the midst of human failure.

Preparing to Lead
- Read and reflect on chapter 6, "God Is Merciful and Gracious."
- Review this plan for the group gathering, and select questions and activities that you will use.
- Gather newsprint and markers, if needed, and prepare to post newsprint sheets on a wall or bulletin board.
- What other questions, issues, or themes occur to you from your reflection?

Gathering
- Provide simple refreshments as people arrive and name tags if still needed.

Opening Worship
Prayer (unison)
Great God, your awesome holiness is exceeded only by your mercy and grace. So many times we have failed to live up to your covenant expectations. We have turned our backs on you and trusted instead in our own ingenuity to secure our lives on our own. We have neglected your guiding presence and set out on our own paths, only to fall flat on our faces. Yet you have not forsaken us and left us to our own devices. You have picked us up and set us back on right paths, and for that, we give you thanks and praise. Amen.

Prayerful, Reflective Reading
- Read Exodus 34:1–9 aloud.
- Invite all to reflect for a few minutes in silence.
- After reflection time, invite all to listen for a word or phrase as the passage is reread and to reflect on that word or phrase in silence.
- Read the passage a third time, asking all to offer a silent prayer following the reading.
- Invite volunteers to share the word or phrase that spoke most deeply to them.

Prayer
Loving God, hear our prayers today as we seek to follow you more faithfully:

(*spoken prayers may be offered*)

Hear us now as we pray together, saying, Our Father . . .

Conversation
- Introduce chapter 6, "God Is Merciful and Gracious." Share observations, reflections, and insights.
- Review the Introduction (pp. 39–40). Share these key points:
  a. The God we meet in Exodus is complex and mysterious—not easy to understand.
  b. Exodus 34:1–9 is a crucial text for understanding the Exodus God; it is a bold affirmation about God's character.
  c. The affirmation is appropriately framed by the story of the golden calf, in which God angrily destroys the original tablets of the Ten Commandments and graciously gives the people a new set of tablets.
- Review "A Basic Theme: God Is Merciful and Gracious" (pp. 40–41). On a sheet of newsprint, write "mercy" and "judgment." Ask:

  What are some examples of God's mercy in chapters 1–33 of Exodus? (Some examples: liberating the people from Egypt; providing food and water in the wilderness.)

  What are examples of God's judgment? (For example, see Exodus 32:30–34, consequences of making the golden calf.)

List the examples on the newsprint. Have someone read aloud Exodus 3:15, the first reference to the name Yahweh ("LORD"), which is used twice in 34:6. Note that Exodus 34:6-7 is an early creed or confessional statement about the character of God. Stand, and read it aloud together. Look up some other Old Testament passages that repeat this creed (e.g., Numbers 14:18; Nehemiah 8:17; Psalms 103:8-14; 145:8; Jonah 4:2). Form several groups, and discuss the first question in For Reflection and Action (pp. 44-45). Have someone from each group report highlights of the discussion.

- Review "The Life of Faith: Bounded by Mercy and Accountability" (pp. 41-43). Ask:

    Can you recall a time when your actions might well have led to retaliation by someone offended but were instead met with mercy?

    Have participants reflect silently on the third question in For Reflection and Action (pp. 44-45). Then have them pair up and share their thoughts. Come back together as a group, and note that God is merciful but also expects accountability. Ask:

    Can you name cases where failure to keep our covenant with God has led to adverse consequences? For example, do reckless environmental actions and inactions, along with the wasteful use of resources, have the potential to harm subsequent generations? Would not such actions be a violation of humans' assigned task to be caretakers of God's world?

- Review "The Church: A Community Bounded by Mercy and Accountability" (pp. 43-44). Look together at Exodus 34:6-7a, noting the "seven expressions" of God's benevolent character: "merciful," "gracious," "slow to anger," "abounding in steadfast love and faithfulness," "keeping steadfast love," and "forgiving iniquity." List these on a sheet of newsprint. Highlight "merciful" and "steadfast love," noting the meaning of the Hebrew words.

    Form several groups, and discuss the second question in For Reflection and Action (pp. 44-45). Ask:

Where are mercy and compassion most needed in the church? In the world?

Have someone from each group report on the discussion. Read aloud the affirmation "God's parental mercy and steadfast devotion to the church hold strong. We are not alone in this matter of being the church."

Conclusion
Read aloud together Psalm 139:1–18 as an affirmation of the merciful presence of God. Form two groups, and have the groups read alternating verses.

Passing the Peace
The peace of Christ be with you.
　　And also with you.
Amen.

Glossary*

Ark of the Covenant. The chest carried by the Hebrews that contained the tablets of the law. It was lost from history, though how and when is unknown.

covenant. A formal agreement or treaty between two parties that established a relationship and in which obligations and mutual responsibilities may be enacted.

Decalogue. (Greek "ten words") The Ten Commandments, which express the will and law of God and deal with relations of humans with God as well as relations of humans with one another.

golden calf. An object erected for worship by the Israelites during the wilderness period. It became an object of idolatry during the time that Moses was receiving the divine law on Mt. Sinai. He ordered it ground into powder and made the people drink it. The result of their idolatry was a plague (Exodus 32).

Passover. The Jewish commemoration of the "passing over" of the angel of death prior to the exodus from Egypt.

steadfast love. (Hebrew *chesed*) A rich term describing God's covenant loyalty, mercy, and loving-kindness.

tabernacle/tent of meeting. The portable tent in which the Hebrews worshiped during the wilderness period of wandering (Exodus 25–27; 36–38).

theophany. An appearance of God that is perceptible to human sight.

Yahweh. Vocalization of a major Old Testament name for God composed of the Hebrew consonants YHWH and usually translated "Lord" in contemporary versions of the Bible.

---

* The definitions here relate to ways these terms are used in this study. Further explorations can be made in other resources, such as Donald K. McKim, *The Westminster Dictionary of Theological Terms*, 2nd ed. (Louisville, KY: Westminster John Knox Press, 2014).

Want to Know More?

Brueggemann, Walter. "The Book of Exodus." In *New Interpreter's Bible*. Nashville: Abingdon Press, 1994.

Fretheim, Terence E. *Exodus*. Interpretation: A Bible Commentary for Teaching and Preaching. Louisville, KY: Westminster John Knox Press, 1991.

Janzen, J. Gerald. "Exodus." In *Westminster Bible Companion*. Louisville, KY: Westminster John Knox Press, 1997.

Yee, Gale A., Hugh R. Page, Jr., and Matthew J. M. Coomber, eds. "The Old Testament and Apocrypha." In *Fortress Commentary on the Bible*. Minneapolis: Fortress Press, 2014.

www.ingramcontent.com/pod-product-compliance
Lightning Source LLC
Chambersburg PA
CBHW050042080526
44586CB00014B/1418